I SPY
CHRISTMAS

A BOOK OF
PICTURE
RIDDLES

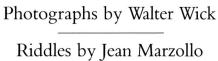

Photographs by Walter Wick

Riddles by Jean Marzollo

Cartwheel
·B·O·O·K·S· ™
SCHOLASTIC INC.

New York   Toronto   London   Auckland   Sydney
Mexico City   New Delhi   Hong Kong   Buenos Aires

For my parents, Betty and Peter Wick

W. W.

Book design by Carol Devine Carson

Text copyright © 1992 by Jean Marzollo.
Illustrations and photographs copyright © 1992 by Walter Wick.
All rights reserved. Published by Scholastic Inc.

SCHOLASTIC, CARTWHEEL BOOKS, and associated logos
are trademarks and/or registered trademarks of Scholastic Inc.

Library of Congress Cataloging-in-Publication Data

Wick, Walter.
    I spy: a book of Christmas riddles / photographs by Walter Wick;
riddles by Jean Marzollo; designed by Carol Devine Carson.
        p.   cm.
    Summary: Rhymes invite the reader to find hidden objects in
photographs of Christmas items.
    ISBN 0-590-45846-9
    1. Picture puzzles—Juvenile literature.   2. Christmas—Juvenile
literature.   [1. Picture puzzles.   2. Christmas—Miscellanea.]
I. Marzollo, Jean.   II. Title.
GV1507.P47W518   1992
793.73—dc20   91-45732
                                                                            CIP
                                                                            AC

Reinforced Library Edition
ISBN-13: 978-0-439-68420-0
ISBN-10: 0-439-68420-X

10 9 8 7   8 9 10 11/0

Printed in Malaysia   46

This edition, March 2005

TABLE OF CONTENTS

Picture riddles fill this book;
Turn the pages! Take a look!

Use your mind, use your eye;
Read the rhymes and play I SPY!

I spy a clock, a bumpy green pickle,
Santa on a sleigh and a face on a nickel;

A frog on a leaf, a chubby teddy bear,

I spy a horse and three glitter shells,
A five-pointed star, and two silver bells;

One golden ring, a little white cat,
A swan and a bear and a thimble hat.

I spy a snowman, three hens in a row,
A drumstick, a rabbit, a small yellow bow;

An almond, a magnet, a sea gull, a chick,
A hammer, five cents, and a wooden toothpick.

I spy a jingle bell, two birds of blue,
A bunny, a star, and Santa's red shoe;

An old-fashioned key, two small striped stones,
A red shoelace, and seven pinecones.

I spy a wagon, five sleds, and a drum,
A smart ladybug, and a stick of gum;

Two snowy mittens, three pairs of gloves,
A monkey named Socks, and two turtledoves.

I spy a house, a drum, and a clock,
Three fat pigs, and a squirrel-tail sock;

18

A string of lights, a belt with a B,
A candy cane, and a broken tree.

I spy a thimble, four birds of red,
Two fuzzy chickens, a gold-trimmed sled;

Three paper clips, an ornament house,
A bottle of glue, and a nutty brown mouse.

I spy a goose, a cat lying down,
A paintbrush, an acorn, a chick, and a clown;

A buffalo nickel, a bird on a block,
Six musical bears, and a key for a lock.

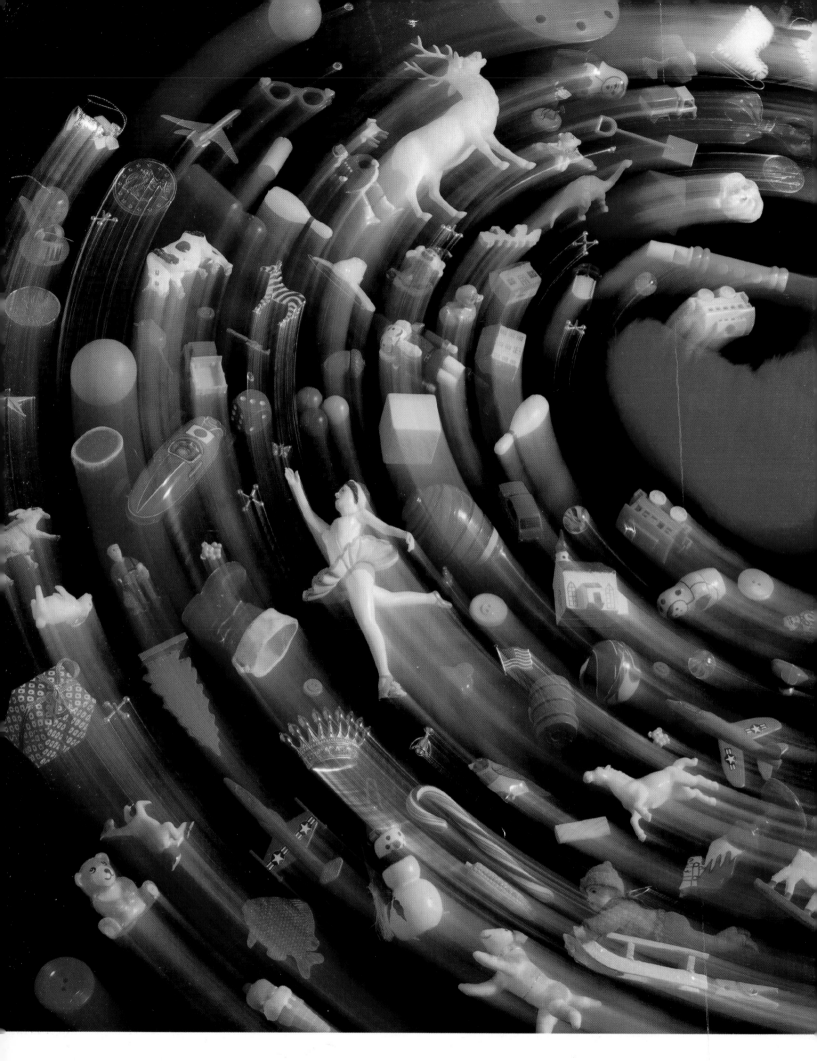

I spy a checker, three candy canes,
A little yellow chick, and seven airplanes;

A pink clothespin, a steeple on a church,
One toy top, and a bird on a perch.

I spy a fish, a brown hatband,
A horse, a cow, and a pointing hand;

A teapot pin, a bell-ringing bear,
A tiny birdhouse, and Santa in a chair.

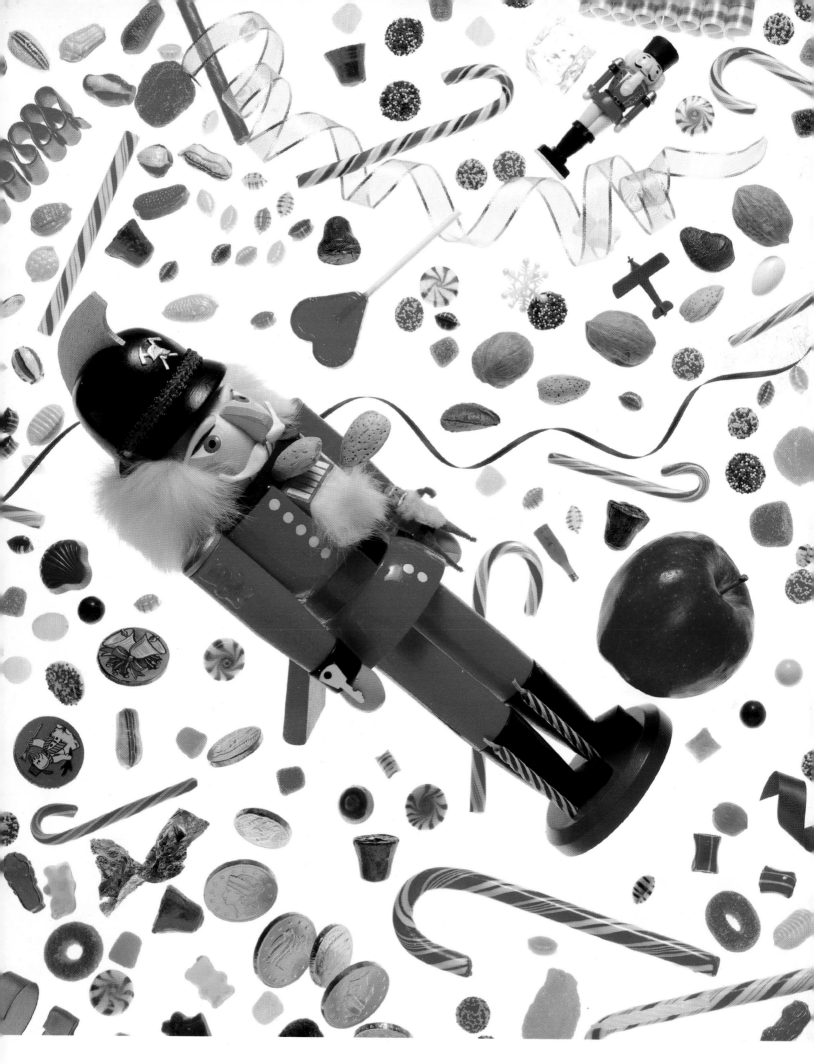

I spy an ice cube, a little twist of lime,
A carrot for a nose, a slim silver dime;

A hatchet at work, a bottle, and a key,
A pinecone, a plane, and a Christmas tree.

I spy a rooster, a Santa with a cane,
The shadow of a star, a car for a train;

Two fancy coaches, a ribbon of blue,
Some musical notes, and JOY 2 U, too.

I spy a glove, a horse, and a gate,
A silver coin, the shadow of a skate;

A shovel, a lamb, a Christmas tree light,
Five jacks, and a dove in the dark silent night.

EXTRA CREDIT RIDDLES

"Find Me" Riddle

Find me with the bears; I sit on their shelf;

I'm in every picture; I'm Santa's _____.

Find the Pictures That Go with These Riddles:

I spy a gumdrop, a skater in red,

Shoes for a baby, and Santa on a sled.

I spy MOTHER, a bear with a broom,

A doll and a phone and a small mushroom.

I spy a chicken, a mouse, and a horn,

An R and a Z, and an ear of corn.

I spy a teacup, an orange tangerine,

Seven candy bears, and a green jellybean.

I spy a rabbit, a spider in the sky,

Seven reindeer, and an angel on high.

I spy a mouse, two kites, and a spoon,

A yellow gumdrop, and an angel with a moon.

I spy a trumpet, an empty nut shell,

Four letter blocks, and the word Noel.

I spy an acorn, a box with a bow,

A fancy gold egg, and a basket in the snow.

I spy a snowman, a colorful clown,

A wintery scene, and a king with a crown.

I spy a pinecone, a tin Christmas tree,

A little gold wrench, and a capital G.

I spy a necktie, candy in a chair,

Two horses that rock, and a hatbox bear.

I spy a streetlight, a soldier in blue,

Four candles, a pan, and a little red shoe.

I spy a ring and a ballet slipper,

Three bells, a truck, and the Little Dipper.

Write Your Own Picture Riddles

There are many more hidden objects and many more possibilities for riddles in this book. Write some rhyming picture riddles yourself, and try them out with friends.

Special Acknowledgments

First of all, we'd like to thank Grace Maccarone, senior editor, and Bernette Ford, editorial director of Cartwheel Books, for their generous enthusiasm and guidance in producing *I Spy: A Book of Picture Riddles* and *I Spy Christmas: A Book of Picture Riddles*. We'd also like to thank Jean Feiwel, Barbara Marcus, Edie Weinberg, John Illingworth, Lenora Todaro, and all the other people at Scholastic who have supported our *I Spy* books.

We'd like to thank our agent, Molly Friedrich of The Aaron M. Priest Literary Agency, for her wit, wisdom, and willingness to solve problems creatively and thoroughly.

We'd like to thank artists Missy Stevens and Tommy Simpson for letting us use their extraordinary collections of antique teddy bears, antique ornaments, and handcrafted Christmas decorations.

And finally, we'd like to thank Dora Jonassen for the cookies, Evan G. Hughes for evergreens, Christopher M. Hayes and Linda Bayette for help with *Santa's Workshop*, Verde Antiques for various props in *Window Shopping*, Katherine O'Donnell and Marianne Alibozak for their photo assistance, and Linda Cheverton-Wick for her superb artistic eye.

Walter Wick and Jean Marzollo

How the Pictures in This Book Were Made

Except for *Antique Teddy Bears*, which was taken at the home of friends, the set for each picture in this book was created by photographer Walter Wick. First, he devised a set (4′ by 8′ or less) for each shot out of wood, shelves, chicken wire, fabric, an old window, pillow stuffing—whatever was needed, even using, in the case of *Silent Night*, baking soda for snow. Next, Wick carefully placed rhyming and non-rhyming objects into the scene, many of which he hid. Then, he lit the scene to achieve desired shadows, depth, and mood. Finally, he photographed the set with an 8″ x 10″ view camera. When satisfied with the artistic quality of the final photo, Wick dismantled the set to make room for the next one. The sets survive only in photos and the reader's imagination.

Walter Wick, the inventor of many photographic games for *Games* magazine, is the photographer of *I Spy: A Book of Picture Riddles*. He is also a free-lance photographer for Scholastic's *Let's Find Out* and *Super Science*. His credits include over 300 magazine and book covers, including *Newsweek, Fortune,* and *Psychology Today*. This is his second book for Scholastic.

Jean Marzollo has written many rhyming children's books including *I Spy: A Book of Picture Riddles, In 1492, Pretend You're a Cat, The Rebus Treasury, The Teddy Bear Book,* and *Close Your Eyes*. She is also the author of books for beginning readers, such as *Cannonball Chris, Soccer Sam, The Green Ghost of Appleville,* and *The Baby Unicorn*. **Carol Devine Carson**, the book designer for *I Spy Christmas* and *I Spy: A Book of Picture Riddles*, is art director for a major publishing house in New York City. She is also the illustrator and designer of *The Rebus Treasury*.